Grandma's Recipes

igloobooks

Published in 2015
by Igloo Books Ltd
Cottage Farm
Sywell
NN6 0BJ
www.igloobooks.com

Food photography and recipe development © Stockfood, The Food Media Agency
Cover images © Stockfood, The Food Media Agency

HUN001 0715
2 4 6 8 10 9 7 5 3 1
ISBN 978-1-78440-691-2

Printed and manufactured in China

Contents

Breakfasts

Nectarine, blueberry and hazelnut porridge

Serves: 4   **Preparation Time:** 5 minutes   **Cooking Time:** 8 minutes

INGREDIENTS

600 ml / 1 pint / 2 ½ cups whole (full-fat) milk, plus extra to serve
125 g / 4 ½ oz / 1 ¼ cups rolled porridge oats
4 tbsp runny honey
a pinch of salt
1 nectarine, stoned and sliced
100 g / 3 ½ oz / ⅔ cup blueberries

3 tbsp toasted hazelnuts (cobnuts), chopped

METHOD

1. Mix the milk with the oats in a saucepan, then stir the mixture over a medium heat until it starts to simmer.

2. Add the honey and a pinch of salt, then reduce the heat to its lowest setting and continue to stir for 4 minutes.

3. Divide the porridge between four bowls and pour over a little extra milk. Top with the nectarine slices, blueberries and hazelnuts.

Quinoa granola with fromage frais

Serves: 4   **Preparation Time:** 20 minutes   **Cooking Time:** 15 minutes

INGREDIENTS

500 ml / 17 ½ fl. oz / 2 cups
   fromage frais
4 tbsp raspberry jam (jelly)
75 g / 2 ½ oz / ½ cup blackberries
75 g / 2 ½ oz / ½ cup blueberries
75 g / 2 ½ oz / ½ cup cherries, halved
   and stoned

For the granola:
100 g / 3 ½ oz / ½ cup uncooked red
   and white quinoa
2 tbsp flaxseeds
4 tbsp pecan nuts, chopped
2 tbsp agave syrup
¼ tsp ground cinnamon

METHOD

1. Preheat the oven to 190°C (170°C fan) / 375F / gas 5 and oil a large non-stick baking sheet.

2. Mix all of the granola ingredients together, then spread them out on the baking sheet.

3. Bake for 15 minutes or until golden brown, then remove from the oven and leave to cool for 5 minutes.

4. Scrape the granola pieces onto a plate with a palette knife and leave to cool to room temperature.

5. Divide the fromage frais between four bowls and top with the jam, fruit and granola.

Cinnamon brioche French toast

Serves: 2   **Preparation Time:** 4 minutes   **Cooking Time:** 4 minutes

INGREDIENTS

2 large eggs
75 ml / 7 ½ fl. oz / ⅓ cup milk
2 tbsp butter
6 thick slices brioche
2 tbsp caster (superfine) sugar
1 tsp ground cinnamon

METHOD

1. Lightly beat the eggs with the milk in a wide, shallow dish and heat the butter in a large frying pan until sizzling.

2. Dip the brioche slices in the egg mixture on both sides until evenly coated, then fry them in the butter for 2 minutes on each side or until golden brown.

3. Mix the sugar with the cinnamon and sprinkle liberally over the French toast.

Banana and poppy seed muffins

Makes: 12   **Preparation Time:** 18 minutes   **Cooking Time:** 15 minutes

INGREDIENTS

3 bananas
100 g / 3 ½ oz / ½ cup soft light
   brown sugar
2 large eggs
125 ml / 4 ½ fl. oz / ½ cup
   sunflower oil
2 tbsp poppy seeds
225 g / 8 oz / 1 ½ cups plain
   (all-purpose) flour

1 tsp bicarbonate of
   (baking) soda

METHOD

1. Preheat the oven to 200°C (180°C fan) / 400F / gas 6 and line a 12-hole cupcake tin with greaseproof paper squares.

2. Mash the bananas with a fork, then whisk in the sugar, eggs, oil and poppy seeds.

3. Sieve the flour and bicarbonate of soda into the bowl and stir just enough to evenly mix all the ingredients together.

4. Divide the mixture between the paper cases, then transfer the tin to the oven and bake for 18 minutes. Test with a wooden toothpick, if it comes out clean, the cakes are done.

5. Transfer the cakes to a wire rack and leave to cool a little before serving.

Blueberry pancakes

Serves: 4   **Preparation Time:** 10 minutes   **Cooking Time:** 30 minutes

INGREDIENTS

250 g / 9 oz / 1 ⅔ cups plain
   (all-purpose) flour
2 tsp baking powder
2 large eggs
300 ml / 10 ½ fl. oz / 1 ¼ cups milk
2 tbsp butter
100 g / 3 ½ oz / ⅔ cup blueberries
maple syrup to serve

METHOD

1. Mix the flour and baking powder in a bowl and make a well in the centre. Break in the eggs and pour in the milk, then use a whisk to gradually incorporate all of the flour from round the outside to form a batter.

2. Melt the butter in a small frying pan, then whisk it into the batter. Put the buttered frying pan back over a low heat. You will need 1 tbsp of batter for each pancake and you should be able to cook four pancakes at a time in the frying pan.

3. Spoon the batter into the pan and cook for 2 minutes or until small bubbles start to appear on the surface of the pancakes.

4. Turn the pancakes over with a spatula and cook the other side until golden brown and cooked through.

5. Repeat until all the batter has been used, keeping the finished batches warm in a low oven.

6. Pile the pancakes onto warm plates, top with blueberries and drizzle with maple syrup.

Mushroom and Cheddar omelette

Serves: 1   **Preparation Time:** 5 minutes   **Cooking Time:** 15 minutes

INGREDIENTS

1 tbsp olive oil
4 tbsp butter
75 g / 2 ½ oz / 1 cup button
    mushrooms, sliced
salt and freshly ground
    black pepper
3 large eggs
5 thin slices Cheddar
chervil leaves to garnish

METHOD

1.   Heat the olive oil and half the butter in a large sauté pan until sizzling.

2.   Add the mushrooms, season with salt and pepper and cook for 10 minutes, stirring occasionally.

3.   Break the eggs into a jug with a pinch of salt and pepper and beat them gently to break up the yolks.

4.   Heat the rest of the butter in a non-stick frying pan until sizzling, then pour in the eggs.

5.   Cook over a medium heat until the egg starts to set around the outside. Use a spatula to draw the sides of the omelette into the centre and tilt the pan to fill the gaps with more egg.

6.   Scatter the mushrooms and Cheddar slices over the top, then continue to cook until the egg is only just set in the centre.

7.   Slide the omelette onto a plate and garnish with chervil leaves.

Eggs Benedict

Serves: 4   **Preparation Time:** 15 minutes   **Cooking Time:** 15 minutes

INGREDIENTS

2 English breakfast muffins, halved
4 large eggs
2 tbsp butter, softened
4 slices prosciutto
1 tbsp chives, finely chopped
freshly ground black pepper

For the hollandaise sauce:
4 tbsp white wine vinegar
1 shallot, finely chopped
1 tsp black peppercorns
1 bay leaf
2 large egg yolks
150 g / 5 ½ oz / ⅔ cup
   butter, melted

METHOD

1.   To make the hollandaise sauce, put the vinegar, shallot, peppercorns and bay leaf in a small saucepan. Boil until the liquid has reduced by half, then strain it into a mixing bowl.

2.   Add the egg yolks and whisk to combine, then set the bowl over a saucepan of simmering water and whisk until pale and thick.

3.   Pour the butter into the bowl in a thin stream, whisking all the time, until it has all been incorporated and the sauce is smooth and thick.

4.   Turn off the heat under the pan – there will be enough heat in the water to keep the sauce warm while you finish the recipe.

5.   Toast the muffin halves and keep warm.

6.   Bring a wide saucepan of water to a gentle simmer. Crack each egg into a cup and pour it smoothly into the water, one at a time.

7.   Simmer gently for 3 minutes, then remove from the pan with a slotted spoon.

8.   Butter the muffin halves and top with the prosciutto slices. Sit a poached egg on top of each one and spoon over the hollandaise. Sprinkle with chives and black pepper and serve immediately.

Hash browns with egg and bacon

Serves: 4   **Preparation Time:** 15 minutes   **Cooking Time:** 35 minutes

INGREDIENTS

450 g / 1 lb / 1 ½ cups waxy potatoes
2 tbsp butter, melted
4 tbsp double (heavy) cream
50 g / 1 ¾ oz / ½ cup Cheddar, grated
salt and freshly ground
    black pepper
4 large eggs
4 rashers bacon, sliced

METHOD

1. Cook the unpeeled potatoes in boiling water for 18 minutes or until a skewer slides in easily. Drain well, then leave to cool completely before peeling.

2. Preheat the oven to 190°C (170°C fan) / 375F / gas 5.

3. Coarsely grate the potatoes, then stir in the butter, cream and cheese and season with salt and pepper.

4. Divide the potato mixture between four individual baking dishes and make a slight hollow in the centres. Break an egg into each one and sprinkle over the sliced bacon.

5. Transfer the dishes to the oven and bake for 15 minutes or until the egg whites have set, but the yolks are still a little runny. Serve immediately.

Baked mushrooms with sausage scramble

Serves: 2   **Preparation Time:** 10 minutes   **Cooking Time:** 30 minutes

INGREDIENTS

2 tbsp butter, melted
4 tbsp wholemeal breadcrumbs
1 tbsp Parmesan, finely grated
salt and freshly ground
    black pepper
4 large portobello mushrooms, stalks
    removed
6 large eggs

2 hot dog sausages, sliced
1 tbsp flat leaf parsley, chopped

METHOD

1. Preheat the oven to 200°C (180°C fan) / 390F / gas 6.

2. Mix the butter, breadcrumbs and Parmesan together and season with salt and pepper. Pack the mixture into the mushrooms, then arrange the mushrooms in a baking dish.

3. Bake the mushrooms for 25 minutes or until tender to the point of a knife.

4. Beat the eggs gently in a saucepan and season with salt and pepper. Set the pan over a low heat and stir continuously until they start to scramble.

5. Add the sliced hot dogs and continue to stir until the eggs are cooked to your liking.

6. Serve the mushrooms on hot plates with the eggs spooned onto the side and garnished with parsley.

Soups and Salads

Tomato and thyme soup

Serves: 4   **Preparation Time:** 5 minutes   **Cooking Time:** 30 minutes

INGREDIENTS

2 tbsp olive oil
1 onion, finely chopped
4 cloves of garlic, crushed
2 tbsp thyme leaves
450 g / 1 lb / 3 cups ripe tomatoes,
    diced
500 ml / 17 ½ fl. oz / 2 cups vegetable
    stock

salt and freshly ground
    black pepper

METHOD

1.   Heat the oil in a saucepan and fry the onion for 8 minutes or until softened.

2.   Add the garlic and half of the thyme to the pan and cook for 2 more minutes, then stir in the tomatoes and vegetable stock and bring to the boil.

3.   Simmer for 20 minutes, then blend until smooth with a liquidiser or stick blender.

4.   Taste the soup and adjust the seasoning with salt and pepper, then ladle into bowls and sprinkle with the rest of the thyme.

Sweet potato and carrot soup

Serves: 6   **Preparation Time:** 10 minutes   **Cooking Time:** 30 minutes

INGREDIENTS

2 tbsp butter
6 spring onions (scallions), chopped
2 cloves of garlic, finely chopped
1 tsp ground coriander (cilantro)
1 large sweet potato, peeled and cubed
2 large carrots, peeled and cubed
1 litre / 1 pint 15 fl. oz / 4 cups
    vegetable stock
2 tbsp coriander (cilantro) leaves

METHOD

1. Heat the butter in a large saucepan and gently fry the spring onions and garlic for 5 minutes to soften.

2. Add the coriander, sweet potato and carrots to the pan and stir to coat in the butter, then pour in the stock and bring to the boil. Reduce the heat a little and simmer for 20 minutes or until the vegetables are tender.

3. Blend the soup until smooth, using a liquidiser or stick blender, then taste and adjust the seasoning.

4. Ladle into bowls and garnish with coriander leaves.

Chilled courgette, mint and feta soup

Serves: 6   **Preparation Time:** 10 minutes   **Cooking Time:** 20 minutes   **Chill Time:** 2 hours

INGREDIENTS

2 tbsp olive oil
1 onion, finely chopped
2 cloves of garlic, finely chopped
4 courgettes (zucchinis), chopped
1 litre / 1 pint 15 fl. oz / 4 cups
    vegetable stock
3 tbsp mint leaves, shredded
100 g / 3 ½ oz / ¼ cup feta, crumbled

salt and freshly ground
    black pepper

METHOD

1.   Heat the oil in a large saucepan, then fry the onion, garlic and courgettes for 10 minutes, stirring occasionally.

2.   Pour in the vegetable stock and bring to the boil, then simmer for 10 minutes.

3.   Stir in half of the mint and feta, then season to taste with salt and pepper. Transfer the soup to a liquidiser and blend until smooth.

4.   Leave the soup to cool to room temperature, then chill for 2 hours.

5.   Ladle the soup into chilled bowls and garnish with the rest of the mint and feta.

Carrot, lentil and coconut soup

Serves: 6   **Preparation Time:** 10 minutes   **Cooking Time:** 40 minutes

INGREDIENTS

3 tbsp vegetable oil
1 onion, finely chopped
2 tsp fresh root ginger, finely chopped
2 cloves of garlic, crushed
2 large carrots, peeled and sliced
200 g / 7 oz / 1 ⅓ cups
    red lentils
1 litre / 1 pint 15 fl. oz / 4 cups
    vegetable stock

200 ml / 7 fl. oz / ¾ cup coconut milk
2 tbsp desiccated coconut

METHOD

1. Heat the oil in a saucepan and fry the onion and ginger for 5 minutes or until softened.

2. Add the garlic and carrots to the pan and cook for 2 minutes, then stir in the lentils and cook for 1 more minute.

3. Pour in the stock and coconut milk and bring to the boil, then reduce the heat a little and simmer for 30 minutes or until the lentils are tender.

4. Ladle two thirds of the soup into a liquidiser and blend until smooth, then stir it back into the saucepan and season to taste with salt.

5. Divide the soup between six warm bowls and garnish with desiccated coconut.

Watercress and mushroom soup

Serves: 4 **Preparation Time:** 10 minutes **Cooking Time:** 15 minutes

INGREDIENTS

2 tbsp olive oil
2 tbsp butter
1 small onion, chopped
2 cloves of garlic, crushed
150 g / 5 ½ oz / 2 cups mushrooms,
 chopped
1 litre / 1 pint 15 fl. oz / 4 cups
 vegetable stock

200 g / 7 oz / 6 cups watercress, washed
 and chopped
salt and freshly ground
 black pepper
2 tbsp chervil, chopped

METHOD

1. Heat the oil and butter in a saucepan and fry the onion for 5 minutes or until softened. Add the garlic and mushrooms to the pan and fry for a further 5 minutes, stirring regularly.

2. Pour in the vegetable stock and bring to the boil, then simmer for 5 minutes.

3. Stir in the watercress, then transfer half of the soup to a liquidiser and blend until smooth. Stir the blended soup back into the saucepan and season to taste with salt and pepper.

4. Ladle the soup into bowls and garnish with chervil.

Smoked haddock chowder

Serves: 4   **Preparation Time:** 15 minutes   **Cooking Time:** 40 minutes

INGREDIENTS

1 litre / 1 pint 15 fl. oz / 4 cups milk
300 g / 10 ½ oz / 1 ¼ cups smoked
   haddock fillet
2 tbsp olive oil
2 tbsp butter
3 leeks, halved and thickly sliced
2 cloves of garlic, crushed
3 medium potatoes, peeled and
   julienned

salt and freshly ground
   black pepper
2 tbsp chives, chopped

METHOD

1. Heat the milk in a saucepan until it starts to simmer, then add the haddock. Simmer gently for 5 minutes, then turn off the heat and leave for a further 5 minutes. Remove the haddock from the pan with a slotted spoon and reserve.

2. Heat the oil and butter in a separate saucepan and fry the leeks for 8 minutes or until softened.

3. Add the garlic and potatoes to the pan and cook for 2 more minutes, then stir in the milk from the haddock and bring to the boil.

4. Simmer for 20 minutes then transfer the soup to a liquidiser and blend until smooth.

5. Pour the soup back into the saucepan and heat gently. Flake the haddock, discarding the skin and bones, and stir it into the soup. Taste and adjust the seasoning with salt and pepper.

6. Ladle the soup into bowls and garnish with chives.

Pumpkin soup with Parmesan tuiles

Serves: 6   **Preparation Time:** 16 minutes   **Cooking Time:** 40 minutes

INGREDIENTS

2 tbsp butter
1 onion, chopped
2 cloves of garlic, crushed
1 small culinary pumpkin, peeled,
    seeded and cubed
1 litre / 1 pint 14 fl. oz / 4 cups
    vegetable stock
4 tbsp double (heavy) cream

salt and freshly ground
    black pepper
3 tbsp Parmesan, grated
1 tbsp poppy seeds

For the Parmesan tuiles:
50 g / 1 ¾ oz / ½ cup Parmesan, grated
2 tbsp poppy seeds

METHOD

1. Heat the butter in a saucepan and fry the onion for 5 minutes or until softened.

2. Add the garlic to the pan and cook for 2 more minutes, then add the pumpkin.

3. Pour in the stock and simmer for 25 minutes or until the pumpkin is tender.

4. Meanwhile, preheat the oven to 180°C (160°C fan) / 350F / gas 4.

5. To make the tuiles, mix the Parmesan with the poppy seeds, then use a round cookie cutter to shape the mixture into 6 circles on a non-stick baking tray.

6. Transfer the tray to the oven and cook for 3 minutes or until the cheese has melted. Leave to cool and harden on the tray for a few minutes, then lift off with a palette knife.

7. Blend the soup in a liquidiser with the cream until smooth, then taste for seasoning, adding salt and pepper as necessary.

8. Ladle the soup into bowls and sprinkle with Parmesan and poppy seeds. Serve with the tuiles.

Tomato and mozzarella salad with sprouting seeds

Serves: 4   **Preparation Time:** 10 minutes

INGREDIENTS

4 large ripe tomatoes
2 mozzarella balls
2 tbsp balsamic vinegar
4 tbsp olive oil
salt and freshly ground
　　black pepper
2 tbsp basil leaves, shredded
1 tbsp baby capers, chopped

100 g / 3 ½ oz / ⅔ cup mixed
　　sprouting seeds

METHOD

1. Cut the tomatoes in half, then slice them across into half-moons.

2. Slice the mozzarella, then arrange on four plates with the tomatoes.

3. Whisk the vinegar and oil together, then season with salt and pepper and stir in the basil and capers.

4. Spoon the dressing over the tomatoes and mozzarella, then add a small pile of sprouting seeds to the centre of each plate.

Rice salad Niçoise

Serves: 4   **Preparation Time:** 20 minutes   **Cooking Time:** 20 minutes

INGREDIENTS

200 g / 7 oz / 1 cup long grain rice
4 large eggs
75 g / 2 ½ oz / ½ cup green beans, cut
into short lengths
½ white onion, quartered
and sliced
75 g / 2 ½ oz / ½ cup canned tuna,
drained and flaked
12 cherry tomatoes, halved

50 g / 1 ¾ oz / ⅓ cup
Niçoise olives
50 g / 1 ¾ oz / 2 cups baby spinach
leaves

For the dressing:
1 clove of garlic, crushed
2 tsp Dijon mustard
1 tsp caster (superfine) sugar

1 lemon, juiced
5 tbsp olive oil
salt and freshly ground
black pepper

METHOD

1. Put the rice in a saucepan and add enough water to cover it by 1 cm (½ in). Bring the pan to the boil, then cover and turn down the heat to its lowest setting.

2. Cook for 10 minutes, then turn off the heat and leave to stand, without lifting the lid, for 10 minutes. Spread the rice out on a plate and leave to cool to room temperature.

3. Meanwhile, cook the eggs in boiling water for 6 minutes, then drain well and plunge into cold water.

4. Cook the beans in boiling, salted water for 4 minutes or until cooked al dente. Drain well, then plunge into cold water. Drain again.

5. Peel the eggs and cut them into quarters. Toss with the rice, beans, onion, tuna, cherry tomatoes, olives and spinach.

6. To make the dressing, whisk the garlic, mustard and sugar together, then whisk in the lemon juice. Add the oil in a thin stream, whisking all the time, until emulsified. Season to taste with salt and pepper, then use to dress the salad.

Chickpea, lentil and cabbage salad

Serves: 6   **Preparation Time:** 10 minutes   **Cooking Time:** 20 minutes

INGREDIENTS

3 tbsp olive oil
1 onion, finely chopped
2 cloves of garlic, crushed
½ tsp chilli (chili) flakes
½ tsp ground cumin
400 g / 14 oz / 1 ⅔ cups canned
    chickpeas (garbanzo beans), drained
200 g / 7 oz / ¾ cup canned lentils,
    drained

200 g / 7 oz / ¾ cup canned tomatoes,
    chopped
½ savoy cabbage, sliced
salt and freshly ground black pepper
lime wedges, pitta bread and mint
    yoghurt to serve

METHOD

1.   Heat the oil in a saucepan and fry the onion and garlic for 5 minutes, stirring occasionally.

2.   Stir in the chilli flakes and cumin, then add the chickpeas, lentils and tomatoes. Add a splash of water, then simmer
     for 15 minutes or until the tomatoes have reduced to a thick sauce.

3.   Meanwhile, cook the cabbage in lightly salted, boiling water for 4 minutes or until cooked al dente. Drain well, then plunge
     into iced water and drain again.

4.   When the chickpeas are ready, season to taste with salt and pepper, then leave them to cool to room temperature and toss
     with the cabbage. Serve with lime wedges for squeezing over and pitta bread and mint yoghurt on the side.

Main Meals

Roast pork with parsnips and pears

Serves: 6   **Preparation Time:** 10 minutes   **Cooking Time:** 1 hour 40 minutes

INGREDIENTS

1.5 kg / 3 lb 5 oz pork loin joint,
  skinned, boned and rolled
4 tbsp olive oil
2 tbsp fresh thyme leaves
salt and freshly ground
  black pepper
6 small parsnips, peeled and
  halved lengthways

3 firm pears, peeled, cored
  and quartered
6 cloves of garlic, unpeeled
200 ml / 7 fl. oz / ¾ cup Marsala

METHOD

1. Preheat the oven to 180°C (160°C fan) / 350F / gas 4.

2. Transfer the pork to a roasting tin lined with greaseproof paper and brush with half of the oil. Sprinkle with thyme and season well with salt and pepper.

3. Roast the pork for 45 minutes.

4. Rub the parsnips, pears and garlic with the rest of the oil and arrange around the pork, then season with salt and pepper.

5. Pour over the Marsala then transfer the tin to the oven and roast for a further 55 minutes, turning the vegetables halfway through.

6. Cover the roasting tin with a double layer of foil and leave to rest for 10 minutes before carving and serving.

Maple-roasted turkey breast with bread sauce

Serves: 4   **Preparation Time:** 10 minutes   **Cooking Time:** 45 minutes

INGREDIENTS

900 g / 2 lb turkey breast
3 tbsp butter, melted
3 tbsp maple syrup
1 tsp Dijon mustard
1 tsp ground mixed spice
flat leaf parsley to garnish

For the bread sauce:
600 ml / 1 pint / 2 ½ cups whole
 (full-fat) milk
1 onion, halved
4 cloves
8 black peppercorns
2 bay leaves
100 g / 3 ½ oz / 1 ⅓ cups fresh
 white breadcrumbs

salt and freshly ground black pepper
¼ tsp ground nutmeg
¼ tsp ground cinnamon

METHOD

1. Preheat the oven to 190°C (170°C fan) / 375F / gas 5.

2. Lay the turkey breast in a roasting tin. Mix together the butter, maple syrup, mustard and mixed spice and brush it over the top.

3. Roast the turkey for 45 minutes or until the juices run clear when pierced with a skewer.

4. Meanwhile, pour the milk into a small saucepan and add the onion, cloves, peppercorns and bay leaves.

5. Bring to a very gentle simmer, then turn the heat down to its lowest setting and infuse for 15 minutes.

6. Pass the mixture through a sieve to remove the aromatics and return the milk to the pan. Stir in the breadcrumbs, then cook over a low heat for 3–4 minutes or until the sauce has thickened.

7. Season to taste with salt and pepper, then spoon the sauce into a bowl and sprinkle with the spices. Carve the turkey breast into slices, garnish with parsley and serve with the sauce on the side.

Fettuccini with walnut meatballs

Serves: 6   **Preparation Time:** 50 minutes   **Cooking Time:** 55 minutes

INGREDIENTS

2 tbsp olive oil
1 onion, finely chopped
2 cloves of garlic, crushed
400 g / 14 oz / 1 ¾ cups canned
   cherry tomatoes
600 g / 1 lb 4 oz / 5 ½ cups dried
   fettuccini
2 tbsp basil leaves, shredded

For the meatballs:
4 tbsp olive oil
1 onion, finely chopped
1 clove of garlic, crushed
250 g / 9 oz / 1 ⅔ cups coarsely
   minced pork
250 g / 9 oz / 1 ⅔ cups sausage meat
50 g / 1 ¾ oz / ⅔ cup fresh white
   breadcrumbs

4 tbsp walnuts, finely chopped
2 tbsp flat leaf parsley, finely chopped
2 tbsp basil leaves, finely chopped
1 egg yolk

METHOD

1. To make the meatballs, heat half of the oil in a large sauté pan and fry the onion for 5 minutes or until softened. Add the garlic and cook for 2 more minutes, stirring constantly, then scrape the mixture into a mixing bowl and leave to cool.

2. Add the mince, sausage meat, breadcrumbs, walnuts, herbs and egg yolk and mix well, then shape into golf-ball-sized meatballs. Chill the meatballs for 30 minutes.

3. Heat the rest of the oil in the sauté pan and sear the meatballs on all sides.

4. To make the sauce, heat the oil in a saucepan and gently fry the onion for 10 minutes to soften. Stir in the garlic and cook for 1 minute, then stir in the tomatoes and simmer for 5 minutes.

5. Tip the sauce into the meatball pan and return to a simmer. Cook gently for 30 minutes or until the meatballs are cooked through and the sauce has reduced a little.

6. Boil the pasta in salted water according to the packet instructions or until al dente. Drain the pasta and divide between six warm bowls, then spoon over the meatballs and sauce and sprinkle with shredded basil.

Individual curried chicken pies

Makes: 4   **Preparation Time:** 30 minutes   **Cooking Time:** 30 minutes

INGREDIENTS

2 tbsp butter
1 onion, finely chopped
50 g / 1 ¾ oz / ½ cup green beans,
    cut into short lengths
2 cloves of garlic, crushed
½ tbsp fresh root ginger,
    finely chopped
2 tsp mild curry powder
1 tsp plain (all-purpose) flour

250 ml / 9 fl. oz / 1 cup coconut milk
200 g / 7 oz / 1 cup cooked chicken
    breast, sliced
1 tbsp coriander (cilantro) leaves,
    finely chopped
salt and white pepper
800 g / 1 lb 12 oz / 2 ¾ cups all-butter
    puff pastry
1 egg, beaten

METHOD

1. Preheat the oven to 200°C (180°C fan) / 400F / gas 6.

2. Heat the butter in a saucepan and gently fry the onion and beans for 5 minutes. Add the garlic and ginger and cook for 2 more minutes.

3. Sprinkle in the curry powder and flour and stir well, then stir in the coconut milk and bubble until it thickens slightly.

4. Add the chicken and coriander to the pan and heat through, then season to taste with salt and white pepper.

5. Roll out half the pastry on a lightly floured surface and use it to line four individual pie dishes. Divide the filling between the pastry cases and brush the rims with water.

6. Roll out the rest of the pastry and top each pie with a pastry lid. Press round the edges to seal, then cut away any excess pastry and use the trimmings to decorate the tops.

7. Brush the pies with beaten egg and bake for 30 minutes or until the pastry is cooked through underneath and golden brown on top.

Ham and mushroom pizza

Makes: 1   **Preparation Time:** 1 hour 45 minutes   **Cooking Time:** 15 minutes

INGREDIENTS

200 g / 7 oz / 1 ⅓ cups strong white
   bread flour, plus extra for dusting
½ tsp easy-blend yeast
1 tsp caster (superfine) sugar
½ tsp fine sea salt
1 tbsp olive oil
3 tbsp tomato pizza sauce
3 slices cooked ham, chopped

4 button mushrooms, sliced
1 mozzarella ball, sliced
½ tsp dried oregano

METHOD

1. Mix together the flour, yeast, sugar and salt and stir the oil into 140 ml / 4 ½ fl. oz / ⅔ cup of warm water. Stir the liquid into the dry ingredients, then knead on a lightly oiled surface for 10 minutes or until smooth and elastic.

2. Leave the dough to rest covered with oiled cling film for 1 hour or until doubled in size.

3. Preheat the oven to 220°C (200°C fan) / 425F / gas 7 and grease a non-stick baking tray.

4. Knead the dough for 2 more minutes, then roll out thinly into a circle and transfer to the baking tray. Spread the dough with the pizza sauce and top with the ham, mushrooms and mozzarella.

5. Sprinkle with oregano and bake for 15 minutes or until the pizza dough is cooked through underneath and the cheese is bubbling.

Individual smoked salmon quiches

Serves: 6   **Preparation Time:** 1 hour   **Cooking Time:** 30 minutes

INGREDIENTS

2 tbsp butter
1 large leek, trimmed
   and sliced
3 large eggs
225 ml / 8 fl. oz / ¾ cup double
   (heavy) cream
salt and freshly ground black pepper
100 g / 3 ½ oz / ⅔ cup smoked
   salmon, sliced

50 g / 1 ¾ oz / ½ cup soft fresh goats'
   cheese, crumbled
2 tbsp chives, chopped

For the pastry:
100 g / 3 ½ oz / ½ cup butter, cubed
200 g / 7 oz / 1 ⅓ cups plain
   (all-purpose) flour

METHOD

1. To make the pastry, rub the butter into the flour until the mixture resembles fine breadcrumbs. Stir in enough cold water to bring the pastry together into a pliable dough and chill for 30 minutes.

2. Preheat the oven to 190°C (170°C fan) / 375F / gas 5.

3. Roll out the pastry on a floured surface and use it to line six individual tart cases. Prick the pastry with a fork, line with greaseproof baking paper and fill with baking beans or rice. Bake the cases for 10 minutes, then remove the paper and baking beans.

4. Meanwhile, heat the butter in a frying pan and fry the leek for 5 minutes or until softened.

5. Gently whisk the eggs with the cream until smoothly combined, then stir in the leeks and season generously with salt and pepper. Pour the filling into the pastry cases and top with the smoked salmon and goats' cheese.

6. Lower the oven temperature to 150°C (130°C fan) / 300F / gas 2 and bake for 20 minutes.or until just set in the centre. Serve hot or cold, garnished with chives.

Stuffed round courgettes

Serves: 6   **Preparation Time:** 20 minutes   **Cooking Time:** 50 minutes

INGREDIENTS

2 tbsp olive oil
1 onion, finely chopped
1 fennel bulb, finely chopped
½ tsp fennel seeds, crushed
2 cloves of garlic, crushed
250 g / 9 oz / 1 cup vegetarian mince
50 g / 1 ¾ oz / ⅔ cup fresh
    white breadcrumbs

4 tbsp Parmesan, finely grated
1 egg yolk
salt and freshly ground
    black pepper
6 round courgettes (zucchinis)

METHOD

1. Preheat the oven to 190°C (170°C fan) / 375F / gas 5.

2. Heat the oil in a frying pan and fry the onion, fennel bulb and fennel seeds for 5 minutes or until softened. Add the garlic and cook for 2 more minutes, stirring constantly, then transfer to a large mixing bowl.

3. Add the vegetarian mince, breadcrumbs, Parmesan and egg yolk and mix everything together to form a stuffing, then season with salt and pepper.

4. Cut off the courgette tops and reserve. Hollow out and discard the insides, then pack the cavities with the stuffing mixture.

5. Put the tops back on the courgettes and bake for 40 minutes or until the stuffing is cooked through to the centre and the courgettes are tender to the point of a knife.

Vegetable moussaka

Serves: 6   **Preparation Time:** 1 hour   **Cooking Time:** 35 minutes

INGREDIENTS

3 tbsp olive oil
1 onion, finely chopped
3 cloves of garlic, crushed
½ cauliflower, cubed
1 orange pepper, sliced
400 g / 14 oz / 2 cups canned
    tomatoes, chopped
1 vegetable stock cube

For the aubergine layer:
3 aubergines (eggplants), cut into
    1 cm (½ in) slices
4 tbsp olive oil
salt and freshly ground
    black pepper

For the topping:
2 tbsp butter
1 ½ tbsp plain (all-purpose) flour
¼ tsp dried oregano
300 ml / 10 ½ fl. oz / 1 ¼ cups
    whole milk
75 g / 2 ½ oz / ¾ cup feta
    cheese, crumbled
4 tbsp Parmesan, finely grated
coriander (cilantro) leaves to garnish

METHOD

1.   Preheat the oven to 200°C (180°C fan) / 400F / gas 6.

2.   Heat the oil in a sauté pan and fry the onion for 10 minutes or until softened. Add the garlic and cook for 2 more minutes.
     Add the cauliflower and orange pepper and stir-fry for 5 minutes.

3.   Add the chopped tomatoes and stock cube and bring to a simmer, then cook over a low heat for 30 minutes.

4.   Meanwhile, brush the aubergine slices with oil and season with salt and pepper, then cook in batches on a smoking hot
     griddle for 2 minutes on each side or until nicely marked.

5.   Melt the butter in a small saucepan. Stir in the flour and oregano then gradually incorporate the milk, stirring continuously
     to avoid any lumps forming. Simmer the sauce until it thickens, then stir in the feta and season to taste with salt
     and pepper.

6.   Line a baking dish with half of the griddled aubergine slices and top with the vegetable sauce. Arrange the rest of the
     aubergine slices on top, then pour over the feta sauce and sprinkle with Parmesan.

7.   Bake the moussaka for 35 minutes or until cooked through and golden brown on top. Garnish with coriander leaves
     before serving.

Stews and Casseroles

Lamb, pepper and fig tagine

Serves: 6   **Preparation Time:** 3 hours 15 minutes   **Cooking Time:** 2 hours

INGREDIENTS

2 tsp ras el hanout spice mix
2 tbsp runny honey
2 tbsp olive oil
800 g / 1 lb 12 oz / 5 ⅓ cups lamb
 shoulder, cut into large chunks
1 onion, quartered and sliced
3 cloves of garlic, finely chopped
150 g / 5 ½ oz / ¾ cup dried
 figs, halved

2 orange peppers, halved
 and sliced
1 bay leaf
1 tbsp fresh thyme leaves
500 ml / 17 ½ fl. oz / 2 cups good
 quality lamb stock
salt and freshly ground
 black pepper

METHOD

1. Stir the ras el hanout, honey and oil together, then massage it into the lamb and leave to marinate for at least 3 hours.

2. Preheat the oven to 160°C (140°C fan) / 325F / gas 3.

3. Stir the rest of the ingredients into the lamb in a tagine or cast iron casserole dish and season well with salt and pepper.

4. Cover the dish and cook in the oven for 2 hours, or until the lamb is tender.

Beef, vegetable and bean casserole

Serves: 6   **Preparation Time:** 20 minutes   **Cooking Time:** 3 hours

INGREDIENTS

900 g / 2 lb / 5 cups beef shin, boned
    and cut into chunks
salt and freshly ground black pepper
2 tbsp olive oil
1 onion, chopped
2 large carrots, cut into chunks
2 bay leaves
800 ml / 1 pint 8 fl. oz / 3 ¼ cups
    beef stock

100 g / 3 ½ oz / ⅔ cup dried broad
    beans (fava beans), soaked overnight
450 g / 1 lb / 3 cups potatoes, peeled
    and cut into large chunks
curly parsley to garnish

METHOD

1. Preheat the oven to 160°C (140°C fan) / 325F / gas 3 and season the beef liberally with salt and pepper.

2. Heat the oil in a large cast iron casserole dish over a high heat, then sear the beef until browned all over.

3. Remove the meat from the pan, lower the heat and add the onions. Cook for 5 minutes, stirring occasionally until softened. Add the carrots and bay leaves and cook for 2 more minutes.

4. Increase the heat, then pour in the stock and bring to a simmer. Return the beef to the pot and add the broad beans, then cover the dish and transfer it to the oven to cook for 2 hours.

5. Give the pot a good stir and add the potatoes, then cover the dish and return it to the oven for a further hour. Season to taste and serve garnished with parsley.

Chunky beef chilli

Serves: 6   **Preparation Time:** 15 minutes   **Cooking Time:** 2 hours

INGREDIENTS

2 tbsp olive oil
1 carrot, sliced
1 celery stick, sliced
1 red chilli (chili),
 finely chopped
2 cloves of garlic, crushed
½ tsp Cayenne pepper
½ tsp ground coriander (cilantro)

450 g / 1 lb / 2 cups braising
 steak, cubed
400 g / 14 oz / 1 ⅔ cups beef stock
400 g / 14 oz / 1 ¾ cups canned kidney
 beans, drained
3 spring onions (scallions), sliced
2 medium tomatoes, diced
1 green pepper, julienned

1 firm avocado, peeled, stoned
 and diced
salt and freshly ground
 black pepper

METHOD

1. Heat the oil in a large saucepan and fry the carrot, celery and chilli for 3 minutes, stirring occasionally.

2. Add the garlic, Cayenne and coriander and cook for 2 minutes, then add the beef.

3. Fry the beef until it starts to brown, then add the stock and bring to a gentle simmer.

4. Cover and simmer gently for 2 hours, stirring occasionally.

5. Stir in the kidney beans, spring onions, tomatoes, pepper and avocado and warm through, then taste for seasoning and add salt and pepper as necessary.

Lamb hotpot

Serves: 6   **Preparation Time:** 25 minutes   **Cooking Time:** 2 hours 30 minutes

INGREDIENTS

1 kg / 2 lb 3 ½ oz / 7 cups boneless
    lamb neck, cubed
3 lamb kidneys, trimmed and quartered
salt and freshly ground
    black pepper
3 tbsp butter
2 tbsp olive oil
2 medium onions, sliced
2 cloves of garlic, crushed

6 sprigs fresh thyme
1 tbsp plain (all-purpose) flour
800 ml / 1 pint 7 fl. oz / 3 ¼ cups
    lamb or chicken stock
1 kg / 2 lb 3 ½ oz / 6 ½ cups potatoes

METHOD

1. Preheat the oven to 160°C (140°C fan) / 325F / gas 3.

2. Blot the lamb neck and kidneys with kitchen paper to ensure they are completely dry, then season liberally with salt and pepper. Melt half the butter with the oil in a frying pan over a high heat, then sear the lamb and kidneys in batches until browned all over.

3. Remove the meat from the pan, lower the heat a little and add the onions. Cook for 5 minutes, stirring occasionally until softened. Add the garlic and thyme and cook for 2 more minutes.

4. Increase the heat and stir in the flour, then incorporate the stock and bring to a simmer. Arrange the lamb and kidneys in a casserole dish and pour over the onion liquor.

5. Slice the potatoes 3 mm thick with a sharp knife or mandolin and arrange them on top of the lamb. Cut the remaining butter into small pieces and dot it over the top of the potatoes, then cover the dish tightly with foil or a lid. Bake for 2 hours 30 minutes, then serve immediately.

Turkey, parsnip and Irish stout casserole

Serves: 6   **Preparation Time:** 20 minutes   **Cooking Time:** 2 hours

INGREDIENTS

900 g / 2 lb / 6 cups turkey meat, cubed
salt and freshly ground
    black pepper
4 tbsp plain (all-purpose) flour
2 tbsp olive oil
1 onion, chopped
4 parsnips, cut into chunks
2 bay leaves
2 star anise

800 ml / 1 pint 8 fl. oz / 3 ¼ cups
    Irish stout

METHOD

1. Preheat the oven to 160°C (140°C fan) / 325F / gas 3. Season the turkey with salt and pepper, then dust with flour.

2. Heat the oil in a large cast iron casserole dish over a high heat, then sear the turkey in batches until browned all over.

3. Remove the meat from the pan, lower the heat and add the onions. Cook for 5 minutes, stirring occasionally until softened. Add the parsnips, bay leaves and star anise and cook for 2 more minutes.

4. Increase the heat then pour in the Irish stout and bring to a simmer. Return the turkey to the pot then cover the dish and transfer it to the oven to cook for 2 hours.

5. Taste the casserole and season with salt and pepper before serving.

Scallop and leek stew

Serves: 2   **Preparation Time:** 5 minutes   **Cooking Time:** 12 minutes

INGREDIENTS

2 tbsp butter
1 leek, trimmed and sliced
2 cloves of garlic, crushed
150 ml / 5 ½ fl. oz / ⅔ cup dry
    white wine
150 ml / 5 ½ fl. oz / ⅔ cup double
    (heavy) cream
8 scallops, halved horizontally
½ tbsp French tarragon, chopped

½ tbsp flat leaf parsley, chopped
salt and freshly ground
    black pepper

METHOD

1. Heat the butter in a saucepan and gently fry the leeks and garlic for 5 minutes or until softened.

2. Turn up the heat and pour in the wine, then simmer until reduced by half. Pour in the cream and lower the heat.

3. When the cream starts to simmer, stir in the scallops and poach gently for 2 minutes or until they just turn translucent.

4. Stir in the herbs and season to taste with salt and pepper, then serve immediately.

Smoked fish casserole

Serves: 6   **Preparation Time:** 15 minutes   **Cooking Time:** 1 hour 30 minutes

INGREDIENTS

2 tbsp olive oil
1 onion, chopped
100 g / 3 ½ oz / ½ cup smoked lardons
1 fennel bulb, julienned
1 large carrot, julienned
450 g / 1 lb / 3 cups waxy potatoes,
   peeled and cut into large chunks
3 bay leaves

a few sprigs of thyme
800 ml / 1 pint 8 oz / 3 ¼ cups
   vegetable stock
175 g / 6 oz / 1 ½ cups small
   Brussels sprouts
1 smoked haddock fillet, skinned and
   cut into chunks

3 smoked mackerel fillets, skinned
   and flaked
salt and freshly ground
   black pepper

METHOD

1.   Preheat the oven to 160°C (140°C fan) / 325F / gas 3.

2.   Heat the oil in a large cast iron casserole dish and fry the onion, lardons and fennel for 10 minutes. Add the carrots, potatoes and herbs, then pour in the stock.

3.   Increase the heat and bring to a simmer, then cover the dish and transfer it to the oven to cook for 1 hour.

4.   Give the pot a good stir and add the sprouts and haddock, then cover the dish and return it to the oven for 30 minutes.

5.   Stir in the mackerel, then season to taste with salt and pepper and serve.

Mini casserole of cod with wild garlic pesto

Serves: 4   **Preparation Time:** 15 minutes   **Cooking Time:** 20 minutes

INGREDIENTS

1 tbsp butter
2 leeks, trimmed and chopped
salt and white pepper
4 portions cod fillet
350 ml / 12 fl. oz / 1 ½ cups fish stock
50 g / 1 ¾ oz / 2 cups wild garlic leaves

For the pesto:
1 ½ tbsp pine nuts, toasted
50 g / 1 ¾ oz / 2 cups wild garlic leaves
25 g / 1 oz / ¼ cup Pecorino,
    finely grated
200 ml / 7 fl. oz / ¾ cup extra virgin
    olive oil

METHOD

1. Preheat the oven to 160°C (140°C fan) / 325F / gas 3.

2. Heat the butter in a frying pan and gently fry the leeks for 5 minutes or until softened. Season with salt and white pepper, then divide between four mini casserole dishes and top with the cod.

3. Pour the stock into the frying pan and bring to the boil, then pour it over the cod and put on the casserole lids.

4. Transfer the casseroles to the oven and cook for 20 minutes.

5. Meanwhile, pound the pine nuts with a pestle and mortar until broken up but not pasty. Add the wild garlic a handful at a time and pound until well pulped, then stir in the cheese and olive oil.

6. When the cod is ready, stir in the wild garlic, then re-cover the pots and let the leaves wilt for 2 minutes.

7. Top the cod with a big spoonful of pesto and serve immediately.

Mediterranean vegetable stew

Serves: 4   **Preparation Time:** 5 minutes   **Cooking Time:** 35 minutes

INGREDIENTS

3 tbsp olive oil
1 onion, chopped
1 yellow pepper, deseeded and cubed
1 red pepper, deseeded and cubed
1 aubergine (eggplant), cubed
3 cloves of garlic, crushed
1 tsp chilli (chili) flakes
a pinch of salt

400 g / 14 oz / 2 cups canned
   tomatoes, chopped
2 tbsp flat leaf parsley, chopped

METHOD

1.   Heat the oil in a large sauté pan and fry the onion and peppers over a low heat for 10 minutes or until softened
     and sweet.

2.   Add the aubergine, garlic and chilli flakes and sauté for 2 minutes. Add a big pinch of salt, then cover the pan and cook
     for 5 more minutes, stirring halfway through.

3.   Uncover the pan, add the tomatoes and stir well. Simmer with the pan partially covered for 15 minutes or until the
     vegetables are tender.

4.   Season to taste with salt and pepper then serve, garnished with parsley.

Tea Time

Strawberry Swiss roll

Serves: 6   **Preparation Time:** 25 minutes   **Cooking Time:** 12 minutes

INGREDIENTS

100 g / 3 ½ oz / ⅔ cup
   self-raising flour
1 tsp baking powder
100 g / 3 ½ oz / ½ cup caster
   (superfine) sugar
100 g / 3 ½ oz / ½ cup butter
2 large eggs
1 tsp vanilla extract

225 g / 8 oz / ⅔ cup strawberry
   jam (jelly)
icing (confectioners') sugar for dusting

METHOD

1.   Preheat the oven to 180°C (160°C fan) / 350F / gas 4 and grease and line a Swiss roll tin with greaseproof paper.

2.   Put the flour, baking powder, sugar, butter, eggs and vanilla extract in a large mixing bowl and whisk together with an electric whisk for 4 minutes or until pale and well whipped.

3.   Spoon the mixture into the tin and spread into an even layer with a palette knife.

4.   Bake for 12 minutes or until the cake is springy to the touch.

5.   When the cake is ready, turn it out onto a sheet of greaseproof paper and peel off the lining paper.

6.   Spread the cake with the jam, then roll it up tightly and leave to cool.

7.   Cut the cake into slices and serve dusted with icing sugar.

Millionaire's shortbread

Serves: 12   **Preparation Time:** 20 minutes   **Cooking Time:** 3 hours 20 minutes

INGREDIENTS

225 g / 8 oz / 1 ½ cups plain
   (all-purpose) flour
75 g / 2 ½ oz / ⅓ cup caster
   (superfine) sugar
150 g / 5 oz / ⅔ cup butter, cubed

For the topping:
400 g / 14 oz canned condensed milk
200 g / 7 oz / 1 ⅓ cups dark chocolate
   (minimum 60 % cocoa solids),
   chopped
50 g / 1 ¾ oz / ½ cup butter

METHOD

1.   Make the caramel layer in advance. Put the unopened can of condensed milk in a saucepan of water and simmer for
     3 hours. Leave the can to cool completely.

2.   Preheat the oven to 180°C (160°C fan) / 350F / gas 4 and line a 20 cm (8 in) square cake tin with greaseproof paper.

3.   Mix together the flour and sugar in a bowl, then rub in the butter. Knead gently until the mixture forms a smooth dough,
     then press it into the bottom of the tin in an even layer.

4.   Bake the shortbread for 20 minutes, turning the tray round halfway through. Leave to cool.

5.   Open the can of condensed milk and beat the caramel until smooth. Spread it over the shortbread and chill for 1 hour.

6.   Put the chocolate and butter in a bowl set over a pan of simmering water and stir together until melted and smooth.

7.   Pour the mixture over the caramel layer and spread it out with a palette knife. Leave to set at room temperature before
     cutting into rectangles.

Carrot tray bake with orange cheesecake cream

Serves: 10   **Preparation Time:** 30 minutes   **Cooking Time:** 40 minutes

INGREDIENTS

175 g / 6 oz / 1 cup soft light
  brown sugar
2 large eggs
150 ml / 5 fl. oz / ⅔ cup sunflower oil
175 g / 6 oz / 1 ¼ cups plain (all-
  purpose) flour
3 tsp baking powder
2 tsp ground cinnamon
1 orange, zest finely grated

200 g / 7 oz / 1 ⅔ cups carrots, washed
  and coarsely grated

For the cream:
110 g / 4 oz / ½ cup cream cheese
55 g / 2 oz / ¼ cup butter, softened
110 g / 4 oz / 1 cup icing
  (confectioners') sugar
1 orange, juiced and zest finely grated

METHOD

1. Preheat the oven to 190°C (170°C fan) / 375F / gas 5 and line a 20 cm x 15 cm (8 in x 6 in) cake tin with greaseproof paper.

2. Whisk the sugar, eggs and oil together for 3 minutes until thick. Fold in the flour, baking powder and cinnamon, followed by the orange zest and carrots.

3. Scrape the mixture into the tin and bake for 40 minutes or until a skewer inserted comes out clean. Transfer the cake to a wire rack and leave to cool completely.

4. To make the cream, beat the cream cheese and butter together with a wooden spoon until light and fluffy, then beat in the icing sugar a quarter at a time. Stir in the orange zest and 2 tsp of juice, then use a whisk to whip the mixture for 2 minutes or until smooth and light.

5. Cut the cake into fingers and serve with a spoonful of the cheesecake cream.

Ginger loaf cake

Serves: 10   **Preparation Time:** 15 minutes   **Cooking Time:** 40 minutes

INGREDIENTS

250 g / 9 oz / 1 ⅔ cups
    self-raising flour
1 tsp bicarbonate of (baking) soda
2 tsp ground ginger
200 g / 8 ½ oz / ⅔ cup golden syrup
125 g / 4 ½ oz / ½ cup butter
125 g / 4 ½ oz / ¾ cup dark
    brown sugar

2 large eggs, beaten
250 ml / 9 fl. oz / 1 cup milk

METHOD

1. Preheat the oven to 180°C (160°C fan) / 355F / gas 4 and grease and line a loaf tin with greaseproof paper.

2. Sieve the flour, bicarbonate of soda and ginger into a bowl.

3. Put the golden syrup, butter and brown sugar in a small saucepan and boil gently for 2 minutes, stirring to dissolve the sugar.

4. Add the butter and sugar mixture to the flour with the eggs and milk and fold it all together until smooth.

5. Scrape the mixture into the prepared tin and bake for 40 minutes or until a skewer inserted comes out clean. Transfer the cake to a wire rack to cool completely before cutting and serving.

Sultana sponge with lemon buttercream

Serves: 10   **Preparation Time:** 35 minutes   **Cooking Time:** 45 minutes

INGREDIENTS

200 g / 7 oz / 1 ⅓ cups
   self-raising flour
200 g / 7 oz / ¾ cup caster
   (superfine) sugar
200 g / 7 oz / ¾ cup butter, softened
4 large eggs
1 tsp baking powder
75 g / 2 ½ oz / ⅓ cup sultanas

To decorate:
100 g / 3 ½ oz / ½ cup butter, softened
200 g / 7 oz / 2 cups icing
   (confectioners') sugar, plus extra
   for dusting
½ lemon, juiced and zest
   finely grated

METHOD

1. Preheat the oven to 180°C (160°C fan) / 350F / gas 4 and grease and line two 20 cm (8 in) round loose-bottomed cake tins.

2. Put all of the cake ingredients in a large mixing bowl and whisk them together with an electric whisk for 4 minutes or until pale and well whipped. Divide the mixture between the two tins and level the tops with a spatula.

3. Bake for 35 minutes or until a toothpick inserted comes out clean. Transfer the cakes to a wire rack to cool completely.

4. To make the buttercream, whisk the butter with an electric whisk, then gradually add the icing sugar. Add the lemon zest and juice and whisk until smooth and well whipped.

5. Spoon the buttercream into a piping bag fitted with a large star nozzle and pipe the icing on top of one of the cakes. Position the other cake on top and dust with icing sugar.

Chocolate chip cookies

Makes: 24   **Preparation Time:** 20 minutes   **Cooking Time:** 15 minutes

INGREDIENTS

225 g / 8 oz / 1 ⅓ cups light
   brown sugar
100 g / 3 ½ oz / ½ cup caster
   (superfine) sugar
175 g / 6 oz / ¾ cup butter, melted
2 tsp vanilla extract
1 egg, plus 1 egg yolk
250 g / 9 oz / 1 ⅔ cups
   self-raising flour

100 g / 3 ½ oz / ⅔ cup dark
   chocolate chips

METHOD

1. Preheat the oven to 160°C (140°C fan) / 325F / gas 3 and line two baking sheets with greaseproof paper.

2. Cream together the two sugars, butter and vanilla extract until pale and well whipped, then beat in the egg and yolk, followed by the flour and chocolate chips.

3. Use an ice cream scoop to portion the mixture onto the prepared trays, leaving plenty of room to spread.

4. Bake the cookies in batches for 15 minutes or until the edges are starting to brown, but the centres are still chewy. Transfer to a wire rack and leave to cool.

Scones with jam and clotted cream

Makes: 12   **Preparation Time:** 25 minutes   **Cooking Time:** 12 minutes

INGREDIENTS

225 g / 8 oz / 1 ½ cups
   self-raising flour
55 g / 2 oz / ¼ cup butter
150 ml / 5 fl. oz / ⅔ cup whole
   (full-fat) milk
1 egg, beaten
200 g / 7 oz / ¾ cup clotted cream
200 g / 7 oz / ¾ cup raspberry jam (jelly)

METHOD

1. Preheat the oven to 220°C (200°C fan) / 425F / gas 7 and oil a large baking sheet.

2. Sieve the flour into a bowl and rub in the butter until the mixture resembles fine breadcrumbs.

3. Stir in enough milk to bring the mixture together into a soft dough.

4. Flatten the dough with your hands on a floured work surface until 2.5 cm (1 in) thick.

5. Use a pastry cutter to cut out 12 circles and transfer them to the prepared baking sheet, then brush with egg.

6. Bake in the oven for 12 minutes or until golden brown and cooked through. Transfer the scones to a wire rack to cool completely.

7. Split open the scones and top each half with clotted cream and raspberry jam.

Raspberry jam

Makes: 700 ml   **Preparation Time:** 5 minutes   **Cooking Time:** 40 minutes

INGREDIENTS

450 g / 1 lb / 2 cups granulated sugar
450 g / 1 lb / 3 cups raspberries
1 lemon, juiced

METHOD

1. Preheat the oven to 110°C (90°C fan) / 225F / gas ¼.

2. Put the sugar in a heatproof bowl and transfer it to the oven along with two glass jars to heat while you start cooking the fruit.

3. Put the raspberries and lemon juice in a large saucepan and cover with a lid. Heat gently for 10 minutes or until they simmer and soften in the juice they produce.

4. Stir in the warmed sugar to dissolve, then increase the heat and boil until the mixture reads 107°C / 225F on a sugar thermometer.

5. Leave the jam to cool and thicken for 10 minutes, then ladle into the prepared jars and seal with clean lids or waxed paper.

Pear and vanilla jam

Makes: 1.2 litres   **Preparation Time:** 5 minutes   **Cooking Time:** 40 minutes

INGREDIENTS

900 g / 2 lbs 5 / cups under-ripe pears
2 lemons, juiced
450 g / 1 lb / 2 cups granulated sugar
2 vanilla pods, split lengthways

METHOD

1. Preheat the oven to 110°C (90°C fan) / 225F / gas ¼ and put in four jars to sterilise.

2. Peel, core and dice the pears, then transfer them to a preserving pan, add the lemon juice and toss well.

3. Add the sugar and vanilla pods and stir well, then stir over a low heat until the sugar dissolves.

4. Increase the heat and boil until the mixture reads 107°C / 225F on a sugar thermometer.

5. Leave the jam to cool and thicken for 10 minutes, then ladle into the prepared jars and seal with clean lids or waxed paper.

Desserts

Treacle, date and oat puddings

Serves: 8   **Preparation Time:** 25 minutes   **Cooking Time:** 25 minutes

INGREDIENTS

250 g / 9 oz / 1 ⅔ cups
   self-raising flour
1 tsp bicarbonate of (baking) soda
100 g / 3 ½ oz / 1 cup rolled
   porridge oats
100 g / 3 ½ oz / ⅓ cup treacle
100 g / 3 ½ oz / ⅓ cup
   golden syrup
125 g / 4 ½ oz / ½ cup butter

125 g / 4 ½ oz / ¾ cup light
   brown sugar
125 g / 4 ½ oz / ⅔ cup medjool
   dates, stoned and quartered
2 large eggs, beaten
250 ml / 9 fl. oz / 1 cup milk

METHOD

1. Preheat the oven to 180°C (160°C fan) / 350F / gas 4 and butter eight individual baking dishes.

2. Sieve the flour and bicarbonate of soda into a bowl and stir in the oats.

3. Put the treacle, golden syrup, butter, brown sugar and dates in a small saucepan and boil gently for 2 minutes, stirring to dissolve the sugar.

4. Add the butter and sugar mixture to the flour with the eggs and milk and fold it all together until smooth.

5. Divide the mixture between the baking dishes and bake for 25 minutes or until a skewer inserted in the middle comes out with just a few damp crumbs sticking to it.

6. Serve hot from the oven.

Apple and cinnamon crumble

Serves: 6   **Preparation Time:** 10 minutes   **Cooking Time:** 45 minutes

INGREDIENTS

2 large cooking apples, peeled, cored
  and chopped
2 eating apples, peeled, cored
  and chopped
4 tbsp caster (superfine) sugar
75 g / 2 ½ oz / ⅓ cup butter
50 g / 1 ¾ oz / ⅓ cup plain
  (all-purpose) flour

25 g / 1 oz / ¼ cup ground almonds
2 tsp ground cinnamon
40 g / 1 ½ oz / ¼ cup light brown sugar

METHOD

1. Preheat the oven to 180°C (160°C fan) / 350F / gas 4.

2. Mix the apples with the sugar and arrange in a foil baking tray.

3. Rub the butter into the flour and stir in the ground almonds, cinnamon and brown sugar. Squeeze a handful of the mixture into a clump and then crumble it over the fruit. Use up the rest of the topping in the same way, then shake the dish to level the top.

4. Bake the crumble for 45 minutes or until the topping is golden brown.

Lemon meringue sponge

Serves: 6   **Preparation Time:** 30 minutes   **Cooking Time:** 35 minutes

INGREDIENTS

110 g / 4 oz / ⅔ cup
  self-raising flour, sifted
110 g / 4 oz / ½ cup caster
  (superfine) sugar
110 g / 4 oz / ½ cup butter, softened
2 large eggs
1 lemon, zest finely grated
225 g / 8 oz / 1 cup lemon curd

For the meringue:
4 large egg whites
110 g / 4 oz / ½ cup caster
  (superfine) sugar

METHOD

1. Preheat the oven to 180°C (160°C fan) / 350F / gas 4 and oil and line a 23 cm (9 in) round cake tin with greaseproof paper.

2. Combine the flour, sugar, butter, eggs and lemon zest in a bowl and whisk together for 2 minutes or until smooth.

3. Scrape the mixture into the tin and level the top, then bake for 25 minutes or until a skewer inserted in the centre comes out clean.

4. Leave the sponge to cool for 10 minutes in the tin, then take it out, remove the greaseproof paper and transfer to a baking tray. Top the sponge with the lemon curd.

5. Whisk the egg whites until stiff, then gradually add the sugar and whisk until the mixture is thick and shiny. Spoon the meringue into a piping bag fitted with a large star nozzle and pipe it on top of the lemon curd.

6. Bake for 10 minutes or until golden brown.

Sultana and marmalade rice pudding

Serves: 5   **Preparation Time:** 5 minutes   **Cooking Time:** 1 hour 30 minutes

INGREDIENTS

50 g / 1 ¾ oz / ¼ cup butter
110 g / 4 oz / ½ cup short grain rice
75 g / 2 ½ oz / ⅓ cup caster
  (superfine) sugar
75 g / 2 ½ oz / ⅓ cup golden sultanas
1 vanilla pod, seeds only
1.2 litres / 2 pints / 4 ½ cups whole
  (full-fat) milk
4 tbsp marmalade

METHOD

1. Preheat the oven to 140°C (120°C fan) / 275F / gas 1.

2. Melt the butter in a cast iron casserole dish and add the rice, sugar, sultanas and vanilla seeds.

3. Stir over a low heat for 2 minutes, then gradually incorporate the milk and bring to a simmer.

4. Cover the casserole dish and bake in the oven for 1 hour 30 minutes.

5. Stir in the marmalade and serve hot or chilled.

Apple sponge pudding

Serves: 6   **Preparation Time:** 10 minutes   **Cooking Time:** 35 minutes

INGREDIENTS

110 g / 4 oz / ⅔ cup self-raising flour,
   sifted
110 g / 4 oz / ½ cup light brown sugar
110 g / 4 oz / ½ cup butter, softened
2 large eggs
1 tsp ground ginger
1 tsp vanilla extract
2 dessert apples, cored and sliced
icing (confectioners') sugar for dusting

METHOD

1.   Preheat the oven to 190°C (170°C fan) / 375F / gas 5 and butter a baking dish.

2.   Combine the flour, sugar, butter, eggs, ground ginger and vanilla extract in a bowl and whisk together for 2 minutes or until smooth.

3.   Scrape the mixture into the baking dish and arrange the apple slices on top.

4.   Transfer the dish to the oven and bake for 35 minutes or until a skewer inserted comes out clean.

5.   Serve the pudding hot from the oven, dusted with icing sugar.

Lime and almond loaf cake

Serves: 8   **Preparation Time:** 10 minutes   **Cooking Time:** 55 minutes

INGREDIENTS

200 g / 7 oz / 1 ⅓ cups self-raising flour
50 g / 1 ¾ oz / ½ cup ground almonds
175 g / 6 oz / ¾ cup caster (superfine) sugar
175 g / 6 oz / ¾ cup butter, softened
3 large eggs
1 lime, juiced and zest finely grated

3 tbsp flaked (slivered) almonds

METHOD

1. Preheat the oven to 160°C (140°C fan) / 325F / gas 3 and line a large loaf tin with greaseproof paper.

2. Combine the flour, ground almonds, sugar, butter, eggs, 1 tbsp of lime juice and the lime zest in a bowl. Whisk together for 2 minutes or until smooth.

3. Scrape the mixture into the tin and level the top, then sprinkle with flaked almonds.

4. Bake for 55 minutes or until a skewer inserted comes out clean. Transfer to a wire rack and leave to cool completely before slicing.

Pineapple tarte tatin

Serves: 6   **Preparation Time:** 10 minutes   **Cooking Time:** 25 minutes

INGREDIENTS

3 tbsp butter, softened and cubed
4 tbsp soft light brown sugar
400 g / 14 oz / 2 cups canned
    pineapple rings, drained
250 g / 9 oz / ¾ cup all-butter
    puff pastry

METHOD

1. Preheat the oven to 220°C (200°C fan) / 425F / gas 7.

2. Dot the butter over the base of a large ovenproof frying pan and sprinkle with sugar, then arrange the pineapple rings on top.

3. Roll out the pastry on a floured surface and cut out a circle the same size as the frying pan.

4. Lay the pastry over the fruit and tuck in the edges, then transfer the pan to the oven and bake for 25 minutes or until the pastry is golden brown and cooked through.

5. Using oven gloves, put a large plate on top of the frying pan and turn them both over in one smooth movement to unmould the tart.

Apricot frangipane tart

Serves: 8   **Preparation Time:** 30 minutes   **Cooking Time:** 35 minutes

INGREDIENTS

450 g / 1 lb / 1 ½ cups puff pastry
225 g / 8 oz / 2 ¼ cups ground
    almonds
225 g / 8 oz / 1 cup butter, softened
225 g / 8 oz / 1 cup caster (superfine)
    sugar
3 large eggs
1 tsp almond extract

3 tbsp plain (all-purpose) flour
12 apricots, stoned and halved

METHOD

1. Preheat the oven to 200°C (180°C fan) / 400F / gas 6 and line a large rectangular tart case with greaseproof paper.

2. Roll out the pastry on a floured surface and use it to line the tart case.

3. Prick the pastry with a fork, line with greaseproof paper and fill with baking beans or rice.

4. Bake for 10 minutes, then remove the paper and baking beans and leave to cool.

5. Whisk together the almonds, butter, sugar, eggs, almond extract and flour until smoothly whipped, then spoon the mixture into the pastry case.

6. Press the apricots into the frangipane, cut side down and bake the tart for 25 minutes or until the frangipane is cooked through and the pastry is crisp underneath.

Milk chocolate fondants

Serves: 6   **Preparation Time:** 50 minutes   **Cooking Time:** 8 minutes

INGREDIENTS

2 tbsp unsweetened cocoa powder
150 g / 6 oz / 1 cup good-quality milk
  chocolate, chopped
150 g / 6 oz / ⅔ cup butter, chopped
85 g / 3 oz / ½ cup caster (superfine)
  sugar
3 large eggs, plus 3 egg yolks
1 tbsp plain (all-purpose) flour

icing (confectioners') sugar
  for dusting

METHOD

1.   Butter six mini casserole dishes and dust the insides with cocoa.

2.   Melt the chocolate, butter and sugar together in a saucepan, stirring to dissolve the sugar. Leave to cool a little, then beat in the eggs and egg yolks and fold in the flour.

3.   Divide the mixture between the dishes and chill for 30 minutes.

4.   Preheat the oven to 180°C (160°C fan) / 350F / gas 4 and put a baking tray in to heat.

5.   Transfer the fondants to the heated baking tray and bake in the oven for 8 minutes.

6.   Leave the fondants to cool for 2 minutes, then sprinkle with icing sugar and serve.

INDEX

Cream, double (heavy)
Hash browns with egg and bacon, 3
Individual smoked salmon quiches, 60
Pumpkin soup with Parmesan tuiles, 40
Scallop and leek stew, 79

Curry powder
Individual curried chicken pies, 56

Dates
Treacle, date and oat puddings, 108

Eggs
Apple sponge pudding, 116
Apricot frangipane tart, 123
Baked mushrooms with sausage scramble, 24
Banana and poppy seed muffins, 15
Blueberry pancakes, 16
Carrot tray bake with orange cheesecake cream, 92
Cinnamon brioche French toast, 12
Eggs Benedict, 28
Full English breakfast, 15
Ginger loaf cake, 95
Hash browns with egg and bacon, 23
Individual smoked salmon quiches, 60
Lemon meringue sponge, 112
Lime and almond loaf cake, 119
Milk chocolate fondants, 124
Mushroom and Cheddar omelette, 19
Rice salad Niçoise, 44
Strawberry Swiss roll, 88
Sultana sponge with lemon buttercream, 96
Treacle, date and oat puddings, 108

Fennel
Fish soup, 53
Smoked fish casserole, 80
Stuffed round courgettes, 63

Figs
Lamb, pepper and fig tagine, 68

Fish
Fish soup, 39
Smoked haddock chowder, 39
Mini casserole of cod with wild garlic pesto, 83
Smoked fish casserole, 80

Flaxseeds
Quinoa granola with fromage frais, 11

Flour, strong white bread
Ham and mushroom pizza, 59

Fromage frais
Quinoa granola with fromage frais, 11

Garlic
Carrot, lentil and coconut soup, 35

Chickpea, lentil and cabbage salad, 47
Chilled courgette, mint and feta soup, 32
Chunky beef chilli, 72
Fettuccini with walnut meatballs, 54
Individual curried chicken pies, 56
Lamb hotpot, 75
Lamb, pepper and fig tagine, 130
Mediterranean vegetable stew, 84
Pumpkin soup with Parmesan tuiles, 40
Rice salad Niçoise, 44
Roast pork with parsnips and pears, 50
Scallop and leek stew, 79
Smoked haddock chowder, 39
Stuffed round courgettes, 63
Sweet potato and carrot soup, 31
Tomato and thyme soup, 28
Vegetable moussaka, 64
Watercress and mushroom soup, 36

Ginger
Apple sponge pudding, 116
Carrot, lentil and coconut soup, 35
Ginger loaf cake, 95
Individual curried chicken pies, 56

Golden syrup
Ginger loaf cake, 95
Treacle, date and oat puddings, 108

Haddock, smoked
Smoked fish casserole, 80
Smoked haddock chowder, 39

Ham
Ham and mushroom pizza, 59

Hazelnuts (cobnuts)
Nectarine, blueberry and hazelnut porridge, 8

Honey
Lamb, pepper and fig tagine, 68
Nectarine, blueberry and hazelnut porridge, 8

Jam (jelly)
Quinoa granola with fromage frais, 11
Scones with jam and clotted cream, 100
Strawberry Swiss roll, 88

Kidneys
Lamb hotpot, 75

Lamb
Lamb chops with apple and broccoli, 101
Lamb hotpot, 75
Lamb, pepper and fig tagine, 68

Leek
Individual smoked salmon quiches, 60
Mini casserole of cod with wild garlic pesto, 83

Scallop and leek stew, 79
Smoked haddock chowder, 39

Lemon
Chicken, apple and red cabbage salad, 47
Lemon meringue sponge, 112
Pear and vanilla jam, 104
Raspberry jam, 103
Rice salad Niçoise, 44
Sultana sponge with lemon buttercream, 96

Lemon curd
Lemon meringue sponge, 112

Lentils
Carrot, lentil and coconut soup, 35
Chickpea, lentil and cabbage salad, 47

Lettuce
Chicken, apple and red cabbage salad, 47

Lime
Lime and almond loaf cake, 119

Mackerel, smoked
Smoked fish casserole, 80

Maple syrup
Maple-roasted turkey breast with bread sauce, 53

Marsala
Roast pork with parsnips and pears, 50

Milk
Blueberry pancakes, 16
Cinnamon brioche French toast, 12
Ginger loaf cake, 95
Maple-roasted turkey breast with bread sauce, 53
Nectarine, blueberry and hazelnut porridge, 8
Scones with jam and clotted cream, 100
Smoked haddock chowder, 39
Sultana and marmalade rice pudding, 115
Treacle, date and oat puddings, 108
Vegetable moussaka, 64

Mushrooms
Baked mushrooms with sausage scramble, 24
Ham and mushroom pizza, 59
Mushroom and Cheddar omelette, 19
Watercress and mushroom soup, 36

Mustard, Dijon
Maple-roasted turkey breast with bread sauce, 53
Rice salad Niçoise, 44

Nectarine
Nectarine, blueberry and hazelnut porridge, 8

Oats
Nectarine, blueberry and hazelnut porridge, 8
Treacle, date and oat puddings, 108